Jesus Followers

Real-Life Lessons *for* Igniting Faith *in the* Next Generation

Books By Anne Graham Lotz and Rachel-Ruth Lotz Wright

Jesus Followers: Real-Life Lessons for Igniting Faith in the Next Generation

Books by Anne Graham Lotz

The Light of His Presence: Prayers to Draw You Near to the Heart of God

Jesus in Me: Experiencing the Holy Spirit as a Constant Companion

The Daniel Prayer: Prayer That Moves Heaven and Changes Nations

Wounded by God's People: Discovering How God's Love Heals Our Hearts

Expecting to See Jesus: A Wake-Up Call for God's People

The Magnificent Obsession: Embracing the God-Filled Life

God's Story

Just Give Me Jesus

Pursuing More of Jesus

Why? Trusting God When You Don't Understand

Heaven: My Father's House (revised)

The Vision of His Glory: Finding Hope in the Revelation of Jesus Christ

Video Bible Studies by Anne Graham Lotz

Jesus in Me (Study Guide and DVD)

The Daniel Prayer (Study Guide and DVD)

Expecting to See Jesus (Study Guide and DVD)

The Magnificent Obsession (Study Guide and DVD)

God's Story (Study Guide and DVD)

Pursuing More of Jesus (Study Guide and DVD)

Heaven: God's Promise for Me (Curriculum DVD and Children's DVD)

The Vision of His Glory (Study Guide and DVD)

For more resources by Anne Graham Lotz, visit
www.annegrahamlotz.org

Jesus
Followers

Real-Life Lessons *for* Igniting Faith
in the Next Generation

STUDY GUIDE + STREAMING VIDEO

FIVE SESSIONS

ANNE GRAHAM LOTZ
RACHEL-RUTH LOTZ WRIGHT

Harper*Christian*
Resources

Jesus Followers Study Guide

© 2022 by Anne Graham Lotz and Rachel-Ruth Lotz Wright

Requests for information should be addressed to:
HarperChristian Resources, 3900 Sparks Dr. SE, Grand Rapids, Michigan 49546

ISBN 978-0-310-15086-2 (softcover)
ISBN 978-0-310-15087-9 (ebook)

HarperChristian Resources titles may be purchased in bulk for church, business, fundraising, or ministry use. For information, please email ResourceSpecialist@ChurchSource.com.

Author is represented by Alive Literary Agency, 5001 Centennial Blvd, #50742, Colorado Springs, CO 80949, www.aliveliterary.com.

First Printing October 2022 / Printed in the United States of America

CONTENTS

ABOUT ANNE GRAHAM LOTZ

CALLED "THE BEST PREACHER IN THE FAMILY" by her father, Billy Graham, Anne Graham Lotz speaks around the globe with the wisdom and authority of years spent studying God's Word.

The *New York Times* named Anne one of the five most influential evangelists of her generation. She's been profiled on *60 Minutes* and has appeared on TV programs such as *Larry King Live, The Today Show,* and *Hannity Live*. Her *Just Give Me Jesus* revivals have been held in more than thirty cities in twelve different countries, with hundreds of thousands of attendees.

Whether a contributor to national newspapers, or a groundbreaking speaker on platforms throughout the world, Anne's aim is clear—to bring revival to the hearts of God's people. And her message is consistent—calling people into a personal relationship with God through His Word and through prayer.

In May 2016, Anne was named the chairperson of the National Day of Prayer Task Force, a position held by only two other women, Shirley Dobson and Vonette Bright, since its inception in 1952.

Anne is a bestselling and award-winning author. Her most recent releases are *Jesus Followers, The Light of His Presence, Jesus in Me, The Daniel Prayer, Wounded by God's People, Fixing My Eyes on Jesus, Expecting to See Jesus,* and her first children's book, *Heaven: God's Promise for Me*.

Anne and her late husband, Danny Lotz, have three grown children and three grandchildren. She is the founder and president of AnGeL Ministries, an independent, nonprofit organization based in Raleigh, North Carolina, that is committed to giving out messages of biblical exposition so God's Word is personal and relevant to ordinary people.

The ministry's name is derived from the initials of Anne Graham Lotz (AGL) and is especially fitting, as angels are messengers of God who go wherever He sends, speak to whomever He directs, and faithfully deliver His Word. AnGeL Ministries serves as the umbrella organization for the diverse ministry of Anne Graham Lotz—including her many books, DVDs, CDs, speaking engagements, and special events.

To learn more about Anne and AnGeL Ministries, visit **www.annegrahamlotz.org**.

ABOUT
RACHEL-RUTH LOTZ WRIGHT

RACHEL-RUTH LOTZ WRIGHT WAS BORN AND RAISED IN RALEIGH, NORTH CAROLINA, the daughter of Anne Graham Lotz and granddaughter of Billy Graham. Following graduation from Baylor University in Waco, Texas, she married Steven Wright, a high school football coach, and now has three daughters: Bell, Sophia, and Riggin.

Rachel-Ruth teaches a weekly women's Bible study that originated at the University of North Carolina and now, through Zoom, reaches thousands worldwide. She also shares God's Word at numerous events around the country. She serves on the board of directors for AnGeL Ministries, in addition to chairing the weekly prayer team that undergirds her mother's ministry.

Her passion for leading children to Jesus and getting them into God's Word compelled her previously to lead monthly missions' chapels at her children's former school; teach middle school children at the Fellowship of Christian Athletes Coaches Camp; and helped to inspire her mother's first children's book, *Heaven: God's Promise for Me*. Her first book, *Jesus Followers*, coauthored with her mother, was released in October 2021.

Rachel-Ruth feels called to encourage others to fall in love with Jesus through the teaching of His Word. To learn more about Rachel-Ruth, visit www.annegrahamlotz.org/about-rachel-ruth-lotz-wright.

PREFACE

THE RACE OF LIFE

Winning a relay race depends not only on the speed of the runners but also on each team member's ability to transfer the baton. If the baton is dropped or even bobbled, precious seconds are wasted, and the race may be lost. If the runner fails to pass the baton, the team is disqualified from the race altogether.

You and I are in a race called life. The Baton is Truth that leads to faith in Jesus Christ. Each generation receives the Baton from the previous generation, runs the race to the best of its ability, then is responsible for passing it smoothly and securely to the next generation.

Is our generation bobbling, or even dropping, the baton? We seem to be experiencing a bankruptcy of moral and spiritual values that threatens to erode our very existence. The flashing-red-light warning for you and me is to beware of . . .

- getting caught up in the way everyone around us is acting,

- indulging in self-pity or self-focus as struggling parents, single or otherwise,

- living for our own selfish desires and happiness,

- conforming to the pressure of the opinions of others,

- succumbing to the intimidation of our cancel-culture,

- and thus neglecting to pass Truth to our children.

As parents, grandparents, and mentors, we must strive to be giants among spiritual dwarfs by receiving, running with, and relaying to the next generation the Baton of Truth that leads to personal faith in Jesus Christ. In order to be successful, it's imperative that we be genuine Jesus Followers ourselves. And that's why we felt compelled to offer you this Bible study.

Our hope is to encourage you to be intentional as you, too, seek to be a Jesus Follower who successfully passes the Baton to the next generation.

Every blessing,

Anne Graham Lotz   Rachel-Ruth Lotz Wright

ABOUT THE STUDY

This study guide is to be used with the video-based course, *Jesus Followers: Real-Life Lessons for Igniting Faith in the Next Generation.* As an integral part of the course, it provides a format for Bible study that serves as the basis for both small-group use (Sunday school classes, women's or men's groups, home or neighborhood studies, one-on-one discipleship) and individual use. This guide will lead you through a series of questions that will enable you to not only discover for yourself the eternal truths revealed by God in the Bible, but also to hear God speaking personally to you through His Word. You then will be prepared to participate in a meaningful time of study and discussion with members of your small group.

PERSONAL STUDY

For each session you will work through five selected passages of Scripture using the 3-Question Study strategy you will learn during the workshop in Session 1. Before you meet with your group, be sure to take the time to reflect and record your personal *Live in Obedient Response to God's Word* statements to share with your group so they can encourage you and hold you accountable.

You will review the lessons, personal applications, and take-aways at your group meeting before you watch the video from Anne and Rachel-Ruth. After each video teaching, there will be group discussion time to learn from one another and share in the experience of how to ignite faith in the next generation.

It is important to complete each personal Bible study before your next session, as this will make the video presentation more meaningful to you during the small-group time. Note that meaningful, daily Bible study will occur if you:

- Set aside a regular place for private devotions.

- Set aside a regular time for private devotions.

- Pray before beginning the day's assignment, asking God to speak to you through His Word.

- Write out your answers for each step, in sequence.

- Make the time to be still and listen, reflecting thoughtfully on your response in the final step.

- Don't rush—it may take time in prayerful meditation on a given passage to discover meaningful lessons and hear the Spirit's whispers.

Spiritual discipline is an essential part of your ability to grow in your relationship with God through knowledge and understanding of His Word. So, take your personal study seriously and allow God to speak to you from His Word. Hearing His voice is thrilling and will make the Bible come alive to you, so get ready to receive blessing after blessing!

GROUP STUDY

In Session 1 of *Jesus Followers*, you will watch the video workshop and be introduced to the 3-Question Study method used in Sessions 2 through 5 personal Bible study. You will be given some time to share insights from your personal Bible study before you and your group watch the video teaching. Space is provided for you to take notes during the video presentation. After the message, you will then have time to discuss the key concepts with your small group using the questions in this guide.

Note: If you are the facilitator for the group, there are additional instructions and resources provided in the facilitator's guide at the back of this book. This guide will help you structure your meeting time, facilitate discussion times, and help lead group members through the key points of the study.

VIDEO SESSION ACCESS

Streaming video access is included with this study guide. There is a streaming video access code and instructions on how to access all of the video sessions on the inside front cover of this study guide.

Simply go to **studygateway.com/redeem** to set up your account and enter your access code to add this study to your new Bible study library. Each time you wish to view a video, simply log in to **studygateway.com/login** and click on the session or study you wish to view. All of your HarperChristian Resources Bible studies with streaming access will be added to your library as you do more studies and redeem the appropriate codes.

INDIVIDUAL COMMITMENT

Remember that the real growth in this study will happen during your quiet times with God. During the group times, you will have the opportunity to process what you have learned with the other members, ask questions, and learn from them as you listen to what God is doing in their lives. In addition, keep in mind that the videos, discussions, and activities in this study are simply meant to tune your heart and your spiritual ears to God's voice so that you can live out what He says as you grow closer to Him.

BIBLE STUDY WORKSHOP

THIS BIBLE STUDY WORKSHOP has a single purpose: to present an approach that will help you learn to listen for God's voice, to grow in your personal relationship with Him, and to have more effective communication with Him through His Word. The following information is introduced in detail in the video presentation. Use this section of the study guide as you view the workshop material. Underline key thoughts and take additional notes as you participate in the workshop. (Note that the passages Anne and Rachel-Ruth use as examples in the video workshop are found on pages 4 and 6.)

WHAT YOU NEED

Before you begin the video workshop for this first session, you will need the following:

- ❏ a Bible
- ❏ this study guide
- ❏ pen or pencil
- ❏ time
- ❏ prayer
- ❏ an open heart

WATCH VIDEO SESSION 1—BIBLE STUDY WORKSHOP (46 MINUTES)

Watch video streaming or on DVD.

Anne and Rachel-Ruth will use this video session to walk you through the following five steps to Bible study with the three questions that are essential to the Bible Study Workshop. They will illustrate how to do this Bible study with **Genesis 17:7.** (See pages 4–5 in your study guide.)

STEPS TO BIBLE STUDY

STEP 1: READ GOD'S WORD. (LOOK AT THE PASSAGE.)

The first step is to read the Bible. At the start of each session in this study guide, you will find the Scriptures listed in a column that you should read during the week. When you have finished reading the passage for the day, move on to Step 2.

STEP 2: WHAT DOES GOD'S WORD SAY? (LIST THE FACTS.)

After reading the passage, make a verse-by-verse list of the outstanding facts. Don't get caught up in the details—just pinpoint the most obvious facts as they appear to you. When you make your list, do not paraphrase the text but use actual words from the passage. Look for the nouns and the verbs.

STEP 3: WHAT DOES GOD'S WORD MEAN? (LEARN THE LESSONS.)

After reading the passage and listing the facts, look for a lesson to learn from each fact.

It may help to ask yourself the following questions:

- Who is speaking?
- What is the subject?
- Where is it taking place?
- When did it happen?

● What can I learn from what is taking place or what is being said?

It may also help to ask yourself: What are the people in the passage doing that I should be doing? Is there a command I should obey? A promise I should claim? A warning I should heed? An example I should follow?

Focus on spiritual lessons.

STEP 4: WHAT DOES GOD'S WORD MEAN IN YOUR LIFE? (LISTEN TO HIS VOICE.)

Although this step will be the most meaningful for you, you can't do it effectively until you complete the first three steps. Rephrase the lessons you found in Step 3 and put them in the form of questions you could ask yourself, your spouse, your child, your friend, your neighbor, or your coworker. As you write the questions, listen for God to speak to you through His Word. Don't get hung up on what you don't understand, but look for the general principles and lessons that can be learned. Remember not to rush this process. It may take you several moments of prayerful meditation to discover meaningful lessons from the Scripture you are reading and hear God speaking to you. The object is not to "get through it," but to develop your personal relationship with God in order to grow in faith and learn to hear the whispers of the Holy Spirit.

STEP 5: WHAT WILL YOU DO ABOUT WHAT GOD HAS SAID? (LIVE IN OBEDIENT RESPONSE TO GOD'S WORD.)

Read the assigned Scripture passages prayerfully, objectively, thoughtfully, and attentively as you listen for God to speak. Note that He may not speak to you through every verse, but He will speak. When He does, record the verse number (if applicable), what it is that God seems to be saying to you, and your response to Him. You might like to date these pages as a means not only of keeping a spiritual journal but also of holding yourself accountable to follow through in obedience. (See pages 4–5 for the example that Anne and Rachel-Ruth demonstrate in the video.)

Afterward, it is your turn to try this method on your own using **Deuteronomy 6:5–7.** (See pages 6–7.)

BIBLE STUDY EXAMPLE

STEP 1 **Read God's Word.** *(Look at the passage.)*	STEP 2 **What Does God's Word Say?** *(List the facts.)*
Passage: Genesis 17:7 *God told Abraham . . .* [7] "I will establish my covenant as an everlasting covenant between me and you and your descendants after you for the generations to come, to be your God and the God of your descendants after you."	**List the outstanding facts—nouns and verbs. Do not paraphrase.** • I will establish my covenant as an everlasting covenant • between me and you and your descendants • to be your God • and the God of your descendants

STEP 3	STEP 4
What Does God's Word Mean?	**What Does God's Word Mean in Your Life?**
(Learn the lessons.)	*(Listen to His voice.)*

Is there a lesson or principle to learn from each fact?

- Our covenant relationship with God is permanent.

- God's relationship with us is not exclusive or elite—He desires every generation to enter into a covenant relationship with Him.

- The covenant is based on a personal relationship with God that begins with me.

- God is committed to our children, grandchildren, and those who come after us.

Rephrase the lessons found in Step 3 into questions.

- If God says the covenant He has made with me is permanent, why would I think I could break or lose it?

- How faithful have I been to tell another generation of God's love and desire to know Him in a personal relationship?

- How obvious is it to my family that I have a personal relationship with God?

- Why would I give up on my children or grandchildren if God is committed to them?

STEP 5
What Will You Do About What God Has Said?
(Live in obedient response to God's Word.)

I will do all I can to tell the next generation that they can enter into a covenant relationship with God.

Date: _____

"YOUR TURN" EXAMPLE

STEP 1 **Read God's Word.** *(Look at the passage.)*	STEP 2 **What Does God's Word Say?** *(List the facts.)*
Passage: Deuteronomy 6:5–7 ⁵ Love the LORD your God with all your heart and with all your soul and with all your strength.	**List the outstanding facts—nouns and verbs. Do not paraphrase.** v. 5
⁶ These commandments that I give you today are to be on your hearts.	v. 6
⁷ Impress them on your children. Talk about them when you sit at home and when you walk along the road, when you lie down and when you get up.	v. 7

STEP 3
What Does God's Word Mean?
(Learn the lessons.)

Is there a lesson or principle to learn from each fact?

STEP 4
What Does God's Word Mean in Your Life?
(Listen to His voice.)

Rephrase the lessons found in Step 3 into questions.

STEP 5
What Will You Do About What God Has Said?
(Live in obedient response to God's Word.)

Date: _____

OUR
WITNESS

SUGGESTED WEEKLY SCHEDULE

DAY 1   3-Question Study—Hebrews 11:4

DAY 2   3-Question Study—John 15:26–27

DAY 3   3-Question Study—Mark 13:11; Revelation 12:11

DAY 4   3-Question Study—1 Peter 3:15

DAY 5   3-Question Study—Acts 1:8

DAY 6   Reflection and Group Study

OUR WITNESS

FROM RACHEL-RUTH'S HEART

ANYONE FAMILIAR WITH BILLY GRAHAM—known to my family as Daddy Bill—knows he shared his faith boldly, without hesitation. Whether witnessing to individuals or preaching in a crowded arena, he did not speak with rehearsed precision. He spoke with passion and conviction because he believed every word he said with every fiber of his being! His deep love for Jesus was always evident in the fire in his piercing blue eyes and the passionate conviction in his familiar voice.

Thousands, even millions, came to faith in Jesus because Daddy Bill's passionate heart for the gospel came through in everything he said and did. Nothing brought him more joy than seeing someone come to Christ! My grandmother, whom we called Tai Tai, told my mom that she and Daddy Bill were once the guests of some friends at a beautiful beach resort. At dinnertime, no one could find Daddy Bill. When Tai Tai went looking for him, she found him behind their building, sharing the gospel with one of the groundskeepers.

My paternal grandfather, whom we simply called Grampa, also shared the gospel with everyone with whom he came in contact, whether a pedestrian on a street corner in New York City, the person riding next to him on the subway, the waiter at the delicatessen he frequented, or one of the hitchhikers he often picked up for the sole purpose of sharing the gospel with them.

One Thanksgiving, he and Gramma were driving down from New York City to spend a week with us. Mom had fixed a beautiful meal to enjoy upon their arrival. We waited and waited. When they finally arrived about eight hours later than expected, we learned Grampa had picked up a hitchhiker, then driven the guy to his destination—six hours out of the way—because Grampa wanted him to know Jesus!

(*RACHEL-RUTH LOTZ WRIGHT* | *JESUS FOLLOWERS* | *Making the Most of Every Opportunity* | *Pages 7–8*)

PERSONAL STUDY

> *By faith Abel brought God a better*
> *offering than Cain did. By faith he was*
> *commended as righteous, when God spoke*
> *well of his offerings. And by faith Abel*
> *still speaks, even though he is dead.*
>
> —HEBREWS 11:4

INTRODUCTION FROM ANNE

OUR WITNESS

The requirement of a blood sacrifice seems to have been clearly communicated to Adam and Eve, because their second son, Abel, chose to approach God in that way and God commended him for it. Abel chose to receive the Baton.

There is no record of Abel teaching or preaching. At this early stage of history, there may have been few other people. Instead, he seems to have silently lived a righteous life that was very different from that of his brother, Cain. Abel's witness has stood the test of time, influencing those who have followed, including you and me.

What caused Abel to choose to be a righteous man? I wonder if it was the positive example of his own father within the home. Did Adam's absolute confidence in the reality of God influence his son?

Surely, although he was now separated from Him, Adam never forgot the touch of God's hand, the sound of God's voice, the expressions on God's face, the authority of God's spoken word. His faith in who God is and what God had said would have been unshakable because he knew God firsthand.

Who has impressed you with his or her confidence in God? What a blessing to have parents and grandparents with confident faith. What a blessing to be a parent or grandparent with confident faith!

What will people think of you when you're gone? What will your grandchildren know about you? Perhaps you see shadows of this ancient generation in your own family tree as you consider those who chose faith and those who did not. Wouldn't it be wonderful if, like Abel, you are remembered throughout generations to come as one whose life bore unmistakable witness to your faith in God? The choice is yours.

The following Bible study has been written to encourage and challenge you to think through the legacy you are building. We pray you will be blessed.

(ANNE GRAHAM LOTZ | JESUS FOLLOWERS | OUR WITNESS | Pages 4–6)

OUR WITNESS

STEP 1	STEP 2
Read God's Word.	**What Does God's Word Say?**
(Look at the passage.)	*(List the facts.)*

Passage: Hebrews 11:4

⁴ By faith Abel brought God a better offering than Cain did.

By faith he was commended as righteous, when God spoke well of his offerings.

And by faith Abel still speaks, even though he is dead.

OUR WITNESS

STEP 3
What Does God's Word Mean?
(Learn the lessons.)

STEP 4
What Does God's Word Mean in Your Life?
(Listen to His voice.)

STEP 5
What Will You Do About What God Has Said?
(Live in obedient response to God's Word.)

Date: _____

OUR WITNESS

STEP 1	STEP 2
Read God's Word.	**What Does God's Word Say?**
(Look at the passage.)	*(List the facts.)*

Passage: John 15:26–27

26 "When the Advocate comes, whom I will send to you from the Father— the Spirit of truth who goes out from the Father—he will testify about me.

27 And you also must testify, for you have been with me from the beginning.

OUR WITNESS

STEP 3
What Does God's Word Mean?
(Learn the lessons.)

STEP 4
What Does God's Word Mean in Your Life?
(Listen to His voice.)

STEP 5
What Will You Do About What God Has Said?
(Live in obedient response to God's Word.)

Date: _____

OUR WITNESS

STEP 1	STEP 2
Read God's Word.	**What Does God's Word Say?**
(Look at the passage.)	*(List the facts.)*

Passage: Mark 13:11; Revelation 12:11

Mark 13:11

[11] Whenever you are arrested and brought to trial, do not worry beforehand about what to say. Just say whatever is given you at the time, for it is not you speaking, but the Holy Spirit.

Revelation 12:11

[11] They triumphed over him
by the blood of the Lamb
and by the word of their testimony;
they did not love their lives so much
as to shrink from death.

OUR WITNESS

STEP 3
What Does God's Word Mean?
(Learn the lessons.)

STEP 4
What Does God's Word Mean in Your Life?
(Listen to His voice.)

STEP 5
What Will You Do About What God Has Said?
(Live in obedient response to God's Word.)

Date: _____

OUR WITNESS

STEP 1	STEP 2
Read God's Word.	**What Does God's Word Say?**
(Look at the passage.)	*(List the facts.)*

Passage: 1 Peter 3:15

[15] But in your hearts revere Christ as Lord. Always be prepared to give an answer to everyone who asks you to give the reason for the hope that you have. But do this with gentleness and respect . . .

OUR WITNESS

STEP 3
What Does God's Word Mean?
(Learn the lessons.)

STEP 4
What Does God's Word Mean in Your Life?
(Listen to His voice.)

STEP 5
What Will You Do About What God Has Said?
(Live in obedient response to God's Word.)

Date: _____

OUR WITNESS

STEP 1	STEP 2
Read God's Word.	**What Does God's Word Say?**
(Look at the passage.)	*(List the facts.)*

Passage: Acts 1:8

⁸ But you will receive power when the Holy Spirit comes on you; and you will be my witnesses in Jerusalem, and in all Judea and Samaria, and to the ends of the earth."

OUR WITNESS

STEP 3	STEP 4
What Does God's Word Mean?	**What Does God's Word Mean in Your Life?**
(Learn the lessons.)	*(Listen to His voice.)*

STEP 5

What Will You Do About What God Has Said?

(Live in obedient response to God's Word.)

Date: _____

REFLECTION

Record and journal the following from your study about *Our Witness*—Being a Jesus Follower.

The Scripture that stood out to you:

The lesson that was most meaningful to you:

The commitment you made to *Live in Obedient Response to God's Word*:

Every morning,
ask God to open
your eyes to
someone who
needs Jesus today.

Jesus Followers | Page 14

GROUP STUDY

Welcome to Session 2 of the *Jesus Followers* Bible study! We continue our study discussing Scripture about Our Witness.

NOTE: *You just completed your first session of Personal Bible Study. If the 3-Question Study technique was new to your group, consider taking a few moments sharing thoughts on the experience before you dive into this week's video teaching. If anyone has questions or concerns about the personal study time, it is likely someone else feels the same way. Spend the time now to find resolution and answers together, so the remainder of this study can be productive and fruitful for everyone.*

Review together your Personal Study Days 1–5 on pages 14 to 23.

From Step 3—What lesson did you learn related to your Witness?

From Step 4—What application questions did you ask yourself?

Share one *Live in Obedient Response to God's Word* to which you committed.

From your Personal Study Reflection on page 24.

WATCH VIDEO SESSION 2—OUR WITNESS
(25 MINUTES)

Watch video streaming or on DVD.

Anne and Rachel-Ruth share stories about their family from the personal study of Dr. Billy Graham in Montreat, North Carolina.

Use this space to take notes if you like:

Scripture in This Session
John 15:26–27
Hebrews 11:4
Acts 1:8

GROUP DISCUSSION QUESTIONS

Open your group discussion sharing something in the video teaching that was either striking or was new to you altogether.

Who is someone you know who needs Jesus today?

According to Scripture, who is Jesus? Is He reflected in what you say and the way you live your life?

What in your life needs to change so it's obvious to others that you are a Jesus Follower?

CLOSING PRAYER

Facilitator, read the following prayer over your group.

FROM ANNE'S HEART

Pray with me . . .

IMMANUEL (GOD WITH US[1]),

We worship You as our Immanuel. We have seen Your glory in the face of Jesus Christ, full of grace and truth (John 1:14). **We cannot keep silent!** We worship You! **We shout Your names!** We praise You! We thank You! We glorify You! We love You!

We humbly, boldly ask that You give us the attention of our family, friends, neighbors, coworkers, classmates, even our enemies, **so that they see our example** and . . .

- they want to know You because they know us.
- they place their faith in You because we are trustworthy.
- they believe You because of what we say, and the way we say it.
- they know You love them because we love them.
- they know You can give them victory over sin because we demonstrate it.
- they have hope because we are so genuinely confident.
- they come to You for freedom from the power of sin because we speak the Truth . . . in love.
- they have peace because we are not afraid.
- they look to You as the solution for what's wrong because we are looking to You.

Raise us up to live our lives filled with Your Spirit. By Your grace. In Your power. For Your glory. Until our faith becomes sight and we see You face-to-face! For the glory of Your name. Amen.

(From MAYDAY Prayer Initiative | Day 9 | May 2015)

---

[1] Matthew 1:23

CONTINUE YOUR JOURNEY
AS A JESUS FOLLOWER

Read PART ONE | Our Witness | Pages 1–50 in the *Jesus Followers* book.

MOVING FORWARD

Review the schedule on page 32.

OUR WORSHIP

SUGGESTED WEEKLY SCHEDULE

DAY 1   3-Question Study—Genesis 4:26; Psalm 95:6–7

DAY 2   3-Question Study—John 4:23–24

DAY 3   3-Question Study—Romans 12:1

DAY 4   3-Question Study—Hebrews 13:15

DAY 5   3-Question Study—Revelation 5:13–14

DAY 6   Reflection and Group Study

OUR WORSHIP

FROM RACHEL-RUTH'S HEART

I REMEMBER MANY OTHER OCCASIONS when Tai Tai, my grandmother, set a limit to my complaints. She would certainly listen and had enormous compassion and wisdom. But she also had the discernment to tell when I was in a whiny mood or just feeling sorry for myself. In those moments, she would tilt her head down in order to muster the deepest voice she could croak out and begin singing an old spiritual:

Nobody knows the trouble I've seen.

Nobody knows but Jesus.

Hearing that deep voice come out of such a tiny woman always put a smile on my face. She used her sense of humor and her ability to commiserate with me to gently remind me to talk to Jesus about whatever the issue was and to quit feeling sorry for myself. I've been guilty of impatiently shutting my kids down when I can tell they are feeling sorry for themselves or are just in a whiny mood. Dropping the hammer certainly stops the pity party, but it may not help their hearts recover as quickly as a sense of humor, compassion, and good old-fashioned distraction. Tai Tai was a master at all three!

It's been said that discouragement is the devil's calling card. He loves to use discouragement to divide relationships, halt effective work, and deflate us to the point that we can hardly function. We have to watch out, knowing the enemy is ultimately behind whatever is discouraging us or our loved ones.

Worshipping the Lord is the best way to fight discouragement. Tai Tai showed me three practical ways to do this: Focus on the blessings in my life, carry a song in my heart, and keep a sense of humor to help remove any traces of discouragement.

(RACHEL-RUTH LOTZ WRIGHT | JESUS FOLLOWERS | Fiddlesticks Chapter 11 | Page 80)

PERSONAL STUDY

> *Seth also had a son, and he named him Enosh. At that time men began to call on the name of the* LORD.
>
> GENESIS 4:26

INTRODUCTION FROM ANNE

OUR WORSHIP

An authentic witness is inextricably linked to a heart devoted to worship. Abel effectively passed the Baton of Truth to his little brother, Seth, who then passed it to his son, Enosh. It was during Enosh's lifetime that people began to call on the name of the Lord. The subtle implication is that Enosh in some way helped lead people in worship.

What would have motivated Enosh to worship God? I wonder whether it was the negative example of his Uncle Cain, who would still have been alive in Enosh's lifetime.

While Enosh witnessed the negative example of his Uncle Cain, he also was given a front-row seat to the godly example of his own father, Seth. But God has no grandchildren! While Seth could pass on a godly heritage, Enosh could not inherit a personal relationship with God. That had to be his own choice. And living in the midst of an increasingly godless civilization, Enosh made that choice.

When he did, others seem to have followed his lead. I wonder whether his friends and neighbors worshipped individually. Or did they join Enosh in corporate worship? All we are told in Scripture is that it was during the lifetime of Enosh that "men began to call on the name of the Lord."

Public worship must arise out of a private, intimate, authentic relationship with God, or it can become perfunctory and religious. Just a tradition with rituals to keep.

For worship to be contagious, it must also be personal. From the heart. Based on a vibrant faith, rooted in the Truth.

How would you describe your worship? Is it mechanical or heartfelt? And what does heartfelt worship communicate? What role does it play in effectively passing on the Baton of Truth? Let's find out . . .

(ANNE GRAHAM LOTZ | JESUS FOLLOWERS | OUR WORSHIP | Pages 53–56)

SESSION 3

OUR WORSHIP

STEP 1	STEP 2
Read God's Word.	**What Does God's Word Say?**
(Look at the passage.)	*(List the facts.)*

Passage: Genesis 4:26; Psalm 95:6–7

Genesis 4:26

²⁶ Seth also had a son, and he named him Enosh. At that time people began to call on the name of the LORD.

Psalm 95:6–7

⁶ Come, let us bow down in worship,
  let us kneel before the LORD our
  Maker;

⁷ for he is our God
  and we are the people of his pasture,
  the flock under his care.

OUR WORSHIP

STEP 3
What Does God's Word Mean?
(Learn the lessons.)

STEP 4
What Does God's Word Mean in Your Life?
(Listen to His voice.)

STEP 5
What Will You Do About What God Has Said?
(Live in obedient response to God's Word.)

Date: _____

OUR WORSHIP

STEP 1	STEP 2
Read God's Word.	**What Does God's Word Say?**
(Look at the passage.)	*(List the facts.)*

Passage: John 4:23–24

[23] "Yet a time is coming and has now come when the true worshipers will worship the Father in Spirit and in truth, for they are the kind of worshipers the Father seeks.

[24] God is spirit, and his worshipers must worship in the Spirit and in truth."

OUR WORSHIP

STEP 3
What Does God's Word Mean?
(Learn the lessons.)

STEP 4
What Does God's Word Mean in Your Life?
(Listen to His voice.)

STEP 5
What Will You Do About What God Has Said?
(Live in obedient response to God's Word.)

Date: _____

OUR WORSHIP

STEP 1	STEP 2
Read God's Word.	**What Does God's Word Say?**
(Look at the passage.)	*(List the facts.)*

Passage: Romans 12:1

[1] Therefore, I urge you, brothers and sisters, in view of God's mercy, to offer your bodies as a living sacrifice, holy and pleasing to God—this is your true and proper worship.

OUR WORSHIP

STEP 3
What Does God's Word Mean?
(Learn the lessons.)

STEP 4
What Does God's Word Mean in Your Life?
(Listen to His voice.)

STEP 5
What Will You Do About What God Has Said?
(Live in obedient response to God's Word.)

Date: _____

OUR WORSHIP

STEP 1	STEP 2
Read God's Word.	**What Does God's Word Say?**
(Look at the passage.)	*(List the facts.)*

Passage: Hebrews 13:15

¹⁵ Through Jesus, therefore, let us continually offer to God a sacrifice of praise—the fruit of lips that openly profess his name.

OUR WORSHIP

STEP 3
What Does God's Word Mean?
(Learn the lessons.)

STEP 4
What Does God's Word Mean in Your Life?
(Listen to His voice.)

STEP 5
What Will You Do About What God Has Said?
(Live in obedient response to God's Word.)

Date: _____

OUR WORSHIP

STEP 1	STEP 2
Read God's Word.	**What Does God's Word Say?**
(Look at the passage.)	*(List the facts.)*

Passage: Revelation 5:13–14

[13] Then I heard every creature in heaven and on earth and under the earth and on the sea, and all that is in them, saying: "To him who sits on the throne and to the Lamb be praise and honor and glory and power, for ever and ever!"

[14] The four living creatures said, "Amen," and the elders fell down and worshiped.

OUR WORSHIP

STEP 3
What Does God's Word Mean?
(Learn the lessons.)

STEP 4
What Does God's Word Mean in Your Life?
(Listen to His voice.)

STEP 5
What Will You Do About What God Has Said?
(Live in obedient response to God's Word.)

Date: _____

OUR WORSHIP

REFLECTION

Record and journal the following from your study about *Our Worship*—Being a Jesus Follower.

The Scripture that stood out to you:

The lesson that was most meaningful to you:

The commitment you made to *Live in Obedient Response to God's Word*:

What view of the Bible are you passing down to your children? As your children, your friends, or your coworkers look at your life, what do they see as being important to you?

Jesus Followers | Page 63

GROUP STUDY

W<small>ELCOME TO</small> S<small>ESSION</small> 3 of the *Jesus Followers* Bible study! We continue our study discussing Scripture about Our Worship.

Review together your Personal Study Days 1–5 on pages 36 to 45.

From Step 3—What lesson did you learn related to your Worship?

From Step 4—What application questions did you ask yourself?

Share one *Live in Obedient Response to God's Word* to which you committed.

From your Personal Study Reflection on page 46.

WATCH VIDEO SESSION 3—OUR WORSHIP
(24 MINUTES)

Watch video streaming or on DVD.

Anne and Rachel-Ruth share stories from the front lawn of the Graham family home in Montreat, North Carolina.

Use this space to take notes if you like:

Scripture in This Session
Genesis 4:25–26
Matthew 17:1–2

GROUP DISCUSSION QUESTIONS

Open your group discussion by sharing something in the video teaching that was either striking or was new to you altogether.

What view of the Bible are you passing down to your children?

As your children, your friends, or your coworkers look at your life, what do they see as being important to you?

What priorities need to change for you to spend daily time in the Word, setting your spiritual compass, and gaining perspective for each new day?

CLOSING PRAYER

Facilitator, read the following prayer over your group.

FROM ANNE'S HEART

Pray with me . . .

We worship You, great God of Creation, as Elohim, the Strong One.

You were in the beginning. You will be at the end. You always have been and You always will be. You are the Creator who brings forth something out of nothing, who formed man from dust, who turns darkness into light, who makes the world turn, who sustains all things by Your powerful word (Hebrews 1:1–3).

We worship You alone.

As we plunge into spiritual and moral darkness,

You are our Light.

In our weakness,

You are our Strength.

As we grieve over lost values and lost loved ones,

You are our Comfort.

In these days of desperation and confusion,

We look to You, and You alone.

Hear our prayers as we come to You in the name of Jesus.

For the glory of Your name. Amen.

(From MAYDAY Prayer Initiative | Day 1 | May 2015)

CONTINUE YOUR JOURNEY
AS A JESUS FOLLOWER

Read PART TWO | Our Worship | Pages 51–98 in the *Jesus Followers* book.

MOVING FORWARD

Review the schedule on page 54.

OUR WALK

SUGGESTED WEEKLY SCHEDULE

DAY 1   3-Question Study—Genesis 5:21–24

DAY 2   3-Question Study—Joshua 1:8–9

DAY 3   3-Question Study—Micah 6:8

DAY 4   3-Question Study—1 John 1:6–7

DAY 5   3-Question Study—1 Thessalonians 2:11–12

DAY 6   Reflection and Group Study

OUR WALK

FROM RACHEL-RUTH'S HEART

ONE SUNDAY MY MOM INVITED all my brother's friends over for his sixteenth birthday party. She, of course, made homemade chocolate pound cake and her famous hot fudge sauce to serve with ice cream.

I'm guessing Murdock's eyes (my childhood pet cockatiel) tripled in size as he saw the steaming pot of chocolate and recognized an irresistible opportunity. He spread his wings in flight, his feet stretched out for a perfect landing, right in the pot of hot fudge! Mom and I both muffled our screams, and I grabbed Murdock out of the hot fudge and set him in his cage.

We could hear the boys getting ready to round the corner and enter the room. A handful of feathers stuck out of the hot fudge, looking like stalks in a cornfield. With lightning speed, Mom plucked them out, gave the hot fudge a stir, and, after shooting me a wide-eyed smile, turned to greet the first boy who walked into the kitchen. "Hot fudge?" "Yes, please."

I've thought of that story a million times as I've faced stressful, everyday situations with my girls . . . Scenarios like these are inevitable in family life. Each one gives us **a chance to walk out our faith** in real time, demonstrating that our priorities are people rather than appearances, and showing the love of God even in stressful times. When we fail to maintain a positive perspective, letting circumstances rather than our unshakable hope determine our attitude, it's time to consider whether we've fallen out of step with God's priorities.

I always remember Mom's reaction to that chocolate catastrophe. She showed extreme patience with me, with Murdock, and with having to serve "birdie" chocolate. She handled it with a sense of humor and a good old-fashioned quick fix.

As I reflect on that memory, I remind myself that I don't need to let stress get the better of me, not when patience and humor can defuse a situation in seconds. Then I determine once again to do my best to be patient and lighthearted, sending up arrow prayers for help when those little stresses come my way.

And I picture Murdock cleaning his feathers as my brother's friends held out their plates for more hot fudge!

(RACHEL-RUTH LOTZ WRIGHT | JESUS FOLLOWERS | Patience Dipped in Chocolate Chapter 16 | Pages 113–114)

PERSONAL STUDY

> *Enoch walked faithfully with God; then he was no more, because God took him away.*
>
> GENESIS 5:24

INTRODUCTION FROM ANNE

OUR WALK

While we don't know how God motivated Enosh to worship, Enosh did make that choice. And his worship inspired not only his friends and neighbors but also his family to join him. He received the Baton of Truth, expressed it during his lifetime through worship, then passed it to his son, Cainan, who passed it to Mahalalel, who passed it to Jared, who passed it to his son, Enoch, who went one step further in expressing his faith **by walking with God**.

What does it mean to walk with God? It's similar to when I walk with a friend. After we have agreed to a time to meet, then we have two rules as we walk. One rule is that we must walk at the same pace. The second rule is that we must walk in the same direction. Without these two rules, we can't walk together. The same two rules apply to walking with God. We must walk at His pace, which is moment-by-moment obedience to His Word. And we must walk in the same direction, which is surrender to His will. If we don't keep the rules, we can't walk with Him.

Enoch's decision to **walk with God** seems to have been prompted by the awesome responsibility of parenting a baby: "After he became the father of Methuselah, Enoch walked with God." When Enoch held his firstborn baby in his arms and gazed on the chubby, flushed cheeks, rosebud mouth, curling eyelashes, and little fist wrapped tightly around his finger, he must have been overcome with an intense awareness that it was his responsibility to care for his child's physical, emotional, and spiritual well-being. Did he exclaim, "How am I going to raise a godly boy in this decadent culture? I need God!" Whatever his words and emotions in that moment, that's when Enoch began to walk with God.

Whatever your circumstances, *do you have* a deep desire in your heart to draw near to God, to **walk with Him**, to receive His wisdom, strength, and blessing as you seek to ignite faith in the next generation?

Maybe that's one reason you are doing this Bible study. You, too, want to raise your children in the Truth, in knowledge of and reverence for the things of God. If so, walking with God is not an option. You and I must walk with Him moment-by-moment. Day by day.

(ANNE GRAHAM LOTZ | JESUS FOLLOWERS | OUR WALK | Pages 101–102)

OUR WALK

STEP 1	STEP 2
Read God's Word.	**What Does God's Word Say?**
(Look at the passage.)	*(List the facts.)*

Passage: Genesis 5:21–24

²¹ When Enoch had lived 65 years, he became the father of Methuselah.

²² After he became the father of Methuselah, Enoch walked faithfully with God 300 years and had other sons and daughters.

²³ Altogether, Enoch lived a total of 365 years.

²⁴ Enoch walked faithfully with God; then he was no more, because God took him away.

OUR WALK

STEP 3
What Does God's Word Mean?
(Learn the lessons.)

STEP 4
What Does God's Word Mean in Your Life?
(Listen to His voice.)

STEP 5
What Will You Do About What God Has Said?
(Live in obedient response to God's Word.)

Date: _____

OUR WALK

STEP 1	STEP 2
Read God's Word.	**What Does God's Word Say?**
(Look at the passage.)	*(List the facts.)*

Passage: Joshua 1:8–9

[8] "Keep this Book of the Law always on your lips; meditate on it day and night, so that you may be careful to do everything written in it. Then you will be prosperous and successful.

[9] Have I not commanded you? Be strong and courageous. Do not be afraid; do not be discouraged, for the LORD your God will be with you wherever you go."

OUR WALK

STEP 3
What Does God's Word Mean?
(Learn the lessons.)

STEP 4
What Does God's Word Mean in Your Life?
(Listen to His voice.)

STEP 5
What Will You Do About What God Has Said?
(Live in obedient response to God's Word.)

Date: _____

OUR WALK

STEP 1	STEP 2
Read God's Word.	**What Does God's Word Say?**
(Look at the passage.)	*(List the facts.)*

Passage: Micah 6:8

[8] He has shown you, O mortal, what is good. And what does the LORD require of you? To act justly and to love mercy and to walk humbly with your God.

SESSION 4

STEP 3
What Does God's Word Mean?
(Learn the lessons.)

STEP 4
What Does God's Word Mean in Your Life?
(Listen to His voice.)

STEP 5
What Will You Do About What God Has Said?
(Live in obedient response to God's Word.)

Date: _____

OUR WALK

STEP 1	STEP 2
Read God's Word.	**What Does God's Word Say?**
(Look at the passage.)	*(List the facts.)*

Passage: 1 John 1:6–7

⁶ If we claim to have fellowship with
him and yet walk in the darkness, we
lie and do not live out the truth.

⁷ But if we walk in the light, as he is
in the light, we have fellowship with
one another, and the blood of Jesus,
his Son, purifies us from all sin.

OUR WALK

STEP 3	STEP 4
What Does God's Word Mean?	**What Does God's Word Mean in Your Life?**
(Learn the lessons.)	*(Listen to His voice.)*

STEP 5

What Will You Do About What God Has Said?

(Live in obedient response to God's Word.)

Date: _____

OUR WALK

STEP 1	STEP 2
Read God's Word.	**What Does God's Word Say?**
(Look at the passage.)	*(List the facts.)*

Passage: 1 Thessalonians 2:11–12

¹¹ For you know that we dealt with each of you as a father deals with his own children,

¹² encouraging, comforting and urging you to live lives worthy of God, who calls you into his kingdom and glory.

OUR WALK

STEP 3	STEP 4
What Does God's Word Mean?	**What Does God's Word Mean in Your Life?**
(Learn the lessons.)	*(Listen to His voice.)*

STEP 5

What Will You Do About What God Has Said?

(Live in obedient response to God's Word.)

Date: _____

REFLECTION

Record and journal the following from your study about *Our Walk*—Being a Jesus Follower.

The Scripture that stood out to you:

The lesson that was most meaningful to you:

The commitment you made to *Live in Obedient Response to God's Word*:

Pray that God would give you boldness and the words to speak the truth with kindness and grace, regardless of the setting or the person.

Jesus Followers | Page 122

GROUP STUDY

Welcome to Session 4 of the *Jesus Followers* Bible Study! We continue our study discussing Scripture about Our Walk.

Review together your Personal Study Days 1–5 on pages 58 to 67.

From Step 3—What lesson did you learn related to your Walk?

From Step 4—What application questions did you ask yourself?

Share the commitment you made to *Live in Obedient Response to God's Word.*

From your Personal Study Reflection on page 68.

WATCH VIDEO SESSION 4—OUR WALK
(30 MINUTES)

Watch video streaming or on DVD.

Anne and Rachel-Ruth share stories from the living room of the Graham family home in Montreat, North Carolina.

Use this space to take notes if you like:

Scripture in This Session
Genesis 5
Genesis 6:9–8:22

GROUP DISCUSSION QUESTIONS

Open your group discussion sharing something in the video teaching that was either striking or was new to you altogether.

Who has commented positively on the way you have handled stress, sickness, or other troubles?

What did they notice?

Who have you been watching who is walking with Jesus?

What have you noticed about them?

CLOSING PRAYER

Facilitator, read the following prayer over your group.

FROM ANNE'S HEART

Pray with me . . .

We worship You as Immanuel. God with us (Matthew 1:23). With us when we arise. With us when we lie down. With us when we go in. With us when we go out. With us when we **walk**. Our desire is to be with You every moment of every day for the rest of our lives. We want to hear Your voice. Feel Your touch. Know what's on Your mind.

You have promised that if we draw near to You, You will draw near to us (James 4:8). So we choose to draw near. We want to **walk** with You as Enoch did. Faithfully. Consistently. Perseveringly. Until our faith becomes sight and we see You face-to-face.

Therefore, we choose to make time to read Your Word, applying it to our lives, in order to live it out in obedient faith so we can **walk** at Your pace. And we choose to surrender our own will, our own plans, our own goals, our own wants and desires . . . to You. We choose to want what You want more than what we want so that we walk in the same direction in which You are **walking**.

And as we **walk with You**, day by day, impart to our hearts what's on Your heart, that we might pray and work effectively.

For the glory of Your great name . . . Jesus.

Amen.

CONTINUE YOUR JOURNEY AS A JESUS FOLLOWER

Read PART THREE | Our Walk | Pages 99–154 in the *Jesus Followers* book.

MOVING FORWARD

Review the schedule on page 76.

OUR WORK

SUGGESTED WEEKLY SCHEDULE

DAY 1   3-Question Study— Genesis 6:13–14; Genesis 6:22

DAY 2   3-Question Study— Colossians 3:23

DAY 3   3-Question Study— John 9:4

DAY 4   3-Question Study— Matthew 5:14–16

DAY 5   3-Question Study— Hebrews 6:10–12

DAY 6   Reflection and Group Study

OUR WORK

FROM RACHEL-RUTH'S HEART

On TYPICAL SATURDAY MORNINGS IN THE FALL and Winter, my dad would have me out in the yard doing chores. His archnemesis was the pine tree, and we had a bazillion of them in our yard. I can still smell the pine straw and hear his rake pulling at the pine needles that had laid claim to the ground, covering the grass. He always used the big, heavy rake that seemed to tear out the grass along with the pine needles, but I think he hated pine needles so much that it was worth the sacrifice of a few blades of grass. He'd hand me a lightweight rake and assign me a section of the yard. I would end up with a sore back and some blisters on my hands, but working hard to clear out the pine needles gave me a sense of accomplishment.

Years later, after my dad went to Heaven, I gasped when I first visited his gravesite. Right next to his plot stood a big old pine tree, dropping pine cones and pine needles all over. Even as we all stood there, a pine needle fell and nailed me in the head like a carefully-aimed missile. I just knew it had to be Dad's angel causing us to laugh when we were so incredibly sad.

While hard work seemed to come naturally to my dad, I think it actually was ingrained in him from an early age. My dad was not raised to sit around. He was born in 1937, into a generation that knew war, knew what it was to ration food, knew how to stretch a dollar, and knew that everyone, young and old, had to work hard in order to keep a household running. His was not a generation raised on social media and television but one instilled with grit and determination, a generation with the backbone to work thirty years in one job whether or not they liked it. And if they lost a job, they would immediately find whatever work they could to provide for their families.

We mimic so much of what we see exemplified by our parents. I know my dad's work ethic was a reflection of his own parents, who worked hard their entire lives.

(RACHEL-RUTH LOTZ WRIGHT | JESUS FOLLOWERS | Hard Work | Pages 171–172)

PERSONAL STUDY

> *By faith Noah, when warned about
> things not yet seen, in holy fear
> built an ark to save his family.*
>
> HEBREWS 11:7

INTRODUCTION FROM ANNE

OUR WORK

Noah received the Baton, and, praise God, not only did he witness, worship, and walk with God; **he also worked for God**. Have you ever stopped to think about what would have happened had Noah been too busy, too tired, too apathetic, or too self-absorbed to work for God? Without his work, you and I wouldn't be here today! **His work for God** is of legendary proportions. Even those unfamiliar with the rest of the Bible know about Noah and his work.

As Noah walked with God, he learned that not only judgment but also salvation was on God's mind. The impending judgment would fall on the entire world, but in His mercy, God wanted to offer salvation to those who would accept it. He told Noah to build an ark. And Noah did exactly what God told him to do.

What courage it must have taken for Noah to **do God's work** in front of the whole wicked world. Added to what was surely a barrage of criticism would have been persecution. The New Testament tells us that Noah was a preacher of righteousness. I wonder if he stood in the door of the ark, warning people that judgment was coming. Did he passionately . . . desperately . . . cry out as he offered them salvation from judgment by inviting them into the safety of the ark? Apparently no one listened or took his preaching seriously. And no one—no one!—believed judgment was coming.

As God had revealed what was on His mind, Noah was not only forewarned but also had clear instructions. He knew how to prepare. He knew what **his specific work** was, and he persevered until the work was finished.

So let's get to work! God has provided an ark, a refuge from the storm of His judgment. But the people all around us don't know that judgment is coming, and they therefore don't know that salvation from judgment is even necessary. We need to warn them. If from time to time it occurs to them that they will be held accountable for their willful wickedness, they don't know how to be saved. **Our work** is to let people know that, yes, judgment is coming, but God offers salvation from His judgment. Just as there was only one door into Noah's ark, there is only one way into salvation from God's judgment: through the cross of Jesus Christ. Our work is to tell people about Jesus, to pass the Baton of Truth to everyone willing to grab hold and run with it.

Ask God to give you an assignment. **A work to do**. Revealing Him in such a way that others are drawn into the ark of salvation by your example. Don't be afraid to let others know you are **working for Jesus**. Accept the Baton of Truth that we are passing to you through this Bible study, and ask God to use it to encourage and motivate you to **work for Him**.

(ANNE GRAHAM LOTZ | JESUS FOLLOWERS | OUR WORK | Pages 157–162)

OUR WORK

STEP 1	STEP 2
Read God's Word.	**What Does God's Word Say?**
(Look at the passage.)	*(List the facts.)*

Passage: Genesis 6:13–14; 6:22

Genesis 6:13–14

13 So God said to Noah, "I am going to put an end to all people, for the earth is filled with violence because of them. I am surely going to destroy both them and the earth.

14 So make yourself an ark of cypress wood; make rooms in it and coat it with pitch inside and out.

Genesis 6:22

22 Noah did everything just as God commanded him.

OUR WORK

STEP 3	STEP 4
What Does God's Word Mean?	**What Does God's Word Mean in Your Life?**
(Learn the lessons.)	*(Listen to His voice.)*

STEP 5

What Will You Do About What God Has Said?

(Live in obedient response to God's Word.)

Date: _____

OUR WORK

STEP 1	STEP 2
Read God's Word.	**What Does God's Word Say?**
(Look at the passage.)	*(List the facts.)*

Passage: Colossians 3:23

23 Whatever you do, work at it with all
your heart, as working for the Lord,
not for human masters . . .

OUR WORK

STEP 3	STEP 4
What Does God's Word Mean?	**What Does God's Word Mean in Your Life?**
(Learn the lessons.)	*(Listen to His voice.)*

STEP 5

What Will You Do About What God Has Said?

(Live in obedient response to God's Word.)

Date: _____

OUR WORK

STEP 1	STEP 2
Read God's Word.	**What Does God's Word Say?**
(Look at the passage.)	*(List the facts.)*

Passage: John 9:4

⁴ As long as it is day, we must do the works of him who sent me. Night is coming, when no one can work.

OUR WORK

STEP 3
What Does God's Word Mean?
(Learn the lessons.)

STEP 4
What Does God's Word Mean in Your Life?
(Listen to His voice.)

STEP 5
What Will You Do About What God Has Said?
(Live in obedient response to God's Word.)

Date: _____

OUR WORK

STEP 1	STEP 2
Read God's Word.	**What Does God's Word Say?**
(Look at the passage.)	*(List the facts.)*

Passage: Matthew 5:14–16

¹⁴ "You are the light of the world. A town built on a hill cannot be hidden.

¹⁵ Neither do people light a lamp and put it under a bowl. Instead they put it on its stand, and it gives light to everyone in the house.

¹⁶ In the same way, let your light shine before others, that they may see your good deeds and glorify your Father in heaven.

OUR WORK

STEP 3
What Does God's Word Mean?
(Learn the lessons.)

STEP 4
What Does God's Word Mean in Your Life?
(Listen to His voice.)

STEP 5
What Will You Do About What God Has Said?
(Live in obedient response to God's Word.)

Date: _____

OUR WORK

STEP 1 **Read God's Word.** *(Look at the passage.)*	STEP 2 **What Does God's Word Say?** *(List the facts.)*

Passage: Hebrews 6:10–12

[10] God is not unjust; he will not forget your work and the love you have shown him as you have helped his people and continue to help them.

[11] We want each of you to show this same diligence to the very end, so that what you hope for may be fully realized.

[12] We do not want you to become lazy, but to imitate those who through faith and patience inherit what has been promised.

OUR WORK

STEP 3	STEP 4
What Does God's Word Mean?	**What Does God's Word Mean in Your Life?**
(Learn the lessons.)	*(Listen to His voice.)*

STEP 5
What Will You Do About What God Has Said?
(Live in obedient response to God's Word.)

Date: _____

REFLECTION

Record and journal the following from your study about *Our Work*—Being a Jesus Follower.

The Scripture that stood out to you:

The lesson that was most meaningful to you:

The commitment you made to *Live in Obedient Response to God's Word*:

Ask God to give
you an unshakable
commitment to
sharing the hope
of the gospel until
your final breath.

Jesus Followers | Page 197

GROUP STUDY

Welcome to Session 5 of the *Jesus Followers* Bible Study! We continue our study discussing Scripture about Our Work.

Review together your Personal Study Days 1–5 on pages 80 to 89.

From Step 3—What lesson did you learn related to your Work?

From Step 4—What application questions did you ask yourself?

Share one *Live in Obedient Response to God's Word* to which you committed.

From your Personal Study Reflection on page 90.

WATCH VIDEO SESSION 5—OUR WORK
(29 MINUTES)

Watch video streaming or on DVD.

Anne and Rachel-Ruth share stories from the kitchen of the Graham family home in Montreat, North Carolina.

Use this space to take notes if you like:

Scripture in This Session

Genesis 4:25 26
Matthew 17, 6:33
Hebrews 13:15
Romans 12:1
Revelation 4

GROUP DISCUSSION QUESTIONS

Open your group discussion sharing something in the video teaching that was either striking or was new to you altogether.

Pray that God would give you a heart of compassion and open your eyes to the needs He wants you and your family to meet. Who comes to mind?

What assignment has God given you?

CLOSING PRAYER

Facilitator, read the following prayer over your group.

FROM ANNE'S HEART

Pray with me . . .

All-Mighty Warrior, Lion of Judah, Captain of the Armies of Heaven, Director of The Day of the Lord.

Give us strength to persevere until we see You in death or at Your return. In the encroaching darkness, fill us with Your Light that directs people to the living Hope that is found in You. In a world swirling and swarming with demons, teach us to use the Sword effectively while wrapping it in unceasing prayer. In a world of deception, cleanse our lips and give us holy boldness to speak Your truth so that we **share Your Gospel** without compromise. **Make us warriors like You**.

We pray for . . . our nation . . . our church . . . our community . . . our family.

We pray in the name of the Rider on the white horse, whose name is Faithful and True, who one day will return, followed by the armies of Heaven. We pray this in the name of the One who judges with justice and makes war, with eyes of blazing fire. We pray this in the name of the Victorious Warrior who one day will vanquish Satan, and remove all sin, evil, wickedness, rebellion, hatred, injustice, and lies from this planet. We pray in the name of JESUS.

Grant us victory this day . . . in His name and for His glory. Amen.

(From MAYDAY Prayer Initiative | Day 7 | May 2015)

CONTINUE YOUR JOURNEY
AS A JESUS FOLLOWER

Read PART FOUR | Our Work | Pages 155–197 in the *Jesus Followers* book.

PASS IT ON

BILLY AND RUTH GRAHAM passed on the Baton of Truth . . . to Anne Graham Lotz, who passed it to Rachel-Ruth Lotz Wright, who now relays it to you.

Now the passing of the Baton is up to you.

Think about it. The Baton of Truth was received by Adam and Eve face-to-face and then relayed faith-to-faith from generation to generation. But it's the same Baton . . . the same Truth . . . the same good news . . . the same gospel . . . that God loves you! He wants you to know Him in a personal relationship. Your sin has separated you from Him, but you can enter into a relationship with Him through the sacrifice of the Lamb, whose blood was shed on the cross to make atonement for your sin. The only way to safety . . . the only way into God's ark . . . the only way to have a right relationship with God is through the blood of the Lamb, the Son of God, the Lord Jesus Christ. Everyone is invited to enter. Whosoever may come. And when you come, your sins are forgiven. You have the hope of Heaven when you die. You have a right relationship with God. You have eternal life. You have Jesus. That's the gospel.

Now it's up to you: Would you make sure you have received and are firmly gripping the Baton of Truth?

Anne and Rachel-Ruth are praying that God will use this Bible study to give you a vision for everyone within your sphere of influence to experience the same certainty of God's love, forgiveness, and welcome that you have. Then run your race by witnessing for God and worshipping God and walking with God and working for God as you pass the Baton to the next generation!

Don't drop the Baton. Don't even bobble it. It's been passed to you through all the generations of human history. Receive it as the treasure that it is, and then pass it on to someone else.

You are a chosen generation . . .
that you may proclaim the praises of
Him who called you out of darkness
into His marvelous light . . .

1 PETER 2:9 NKJV

GROUP
PRAYER REQUESTS

And pray in the Spirit on all occasions
with all kinds of prayers and requests.
With this in mind, be alert and always
keep on praying for all the Lord's people.

EPHESIANS 6:18

BIBLE STUDY WORKSHOP

For THE BEST EXPERIENCE in facilitating this study, it's important to preview the video for session 1 and complete all the written exercises in this study guide prior to leading your group. Familiarize yourself with the session outline and gather the necessary materials. Pray for the participants by name (if known). Pray Ephesians 1:17–18 for them, that God will open their hearts to His Word, and they will get to know Him better as a result of the Spirit's revelation. We suggest using these videos as a weekly Bible study but they could also be used monthly or whatever would be best suited for your group.

SESSION OUTLINE
(90 MINUTES)

I. Introduction/Opening Prayer (5 minutes)

II. Explanation of Bible Study Sessions (5 minutes)

III. Video Teaching and Group Work (70 minutes)

    A. Opening and Teaching on Steps 1–2 (13 minutes)

    B. Group Work on Steps 1–2 (5 minutes)

    C. Review of Steps 1–2 and Teaching on Step 3 (12 minutes)

    D. Group Work on Step 3 (5 minutes)

    E. Review of Step 3 and Teaching on Step 4 (13 minutes)

    F. Group Work on Step 4 (5 minutes)

IV. Wrapping Up and Next Steps (10 minutes)

INTRODUCTION/OPENING PRAYER
(5 MINUTES)

Take a few moments as this opening session begins to introduce yourself to anyone in the group you do not know and give your contact information. If it can be done quickly, ask the participants to introduce themselves. It may be helpful in a larger group to provide nametags. To save time, you can have the nametags pre-printed with their names on one side, and your name and contact information on the other side. Ensure the participants have a copy of the study guide. Pray that God would use this session to help everyone present to become more effective students and doers of His Word.

EXPLANATION OF BIBLE STUDY SESSIONS
(5 MINUTES)

Explain that this first session in *Jesus Followers* is unique, as Anne will describe a method for studying the Bible that they will use during their personal quiet time throughout the study. During this opening session, which will be approximately 90 minutes in length, the group members will watch the video and complete the work found on pages 4–7.

VIDEO TEACHING AND GROUP WORK
(70 MINUTES)

Show the video, following the instructions given by Anne during the session. Note that you will be stopping the video periodically for the participants to complete each of the steps.

WRAPPING UP AND NEXT STEPS
(10 MINUTES)

Tell the group members that they will begin to explore being a Jesus Follower in sessions 2–5. Refer group members to the Personal Study beginning on page 14, and ask them to complete the studies before the next session. Close your time in prayer.

OUR WITNESS

Preview the video before your meeting and complete all the written exercises in this guide. Familiarize yourself with the session outline and gather the necessary materials. Remember also to pray for the participants who will be attending.

SESSION OUTLINE
(60 MINUTES)

REVIEW OF PERSONAL STUDY (15 MINUTES)

Welcome any new participants, and then refer the group to their notes on pages 14–24. Begin by having several different members share the following:

- The lessons they learned from each verse (Step 3)
- The most meaningful question they wrote out in response to Step 4, citing the verse on which the question was based
- Their outstanding takeaway in Step 5

VIDEO TEACHING (25 MINUTES)

Watch the teaching video for session 2. Refer the group members to page 27 and remind them there is space to take notes.

GROUP DISCUSSION (10 MINUTES)

Refer to the Group Discussion questions on page 28 to stimulate discussion on the topics presented during the video teaching. Ask the group members to share any personal encouragement, challenge, or inspiration they received as they watched.

WRAP UP AND GO DEEPER (10 MINUTES)

Conclude by praying over your group. Review the schedule on page 32. Remind them to complete the personal studies before the next session.

OUR
WORSHIP

PREVIEW THE VIDEO before your meeting and complete all the written exercises in this guide. Familiarize yourself with the session outline and gather the necessary materials. Remember also to pray for the participants who will be attending.

SESSION OUTLINE
(60 MINUTES)

REVIEW OF PERSONAL STUDY (15 MINUTES)

Welcome any new participants, and then refer the group to their notes on pages 36–46. Begin by having several different members share the following:

- The lessons they learned from each verse (Step 3)
- The most meaningful question they wrote out in response to Step 4, citing the verse on which the question was based
- Their outstanding takeaway in Step 5

VIDEO TEACHING (24 MINUTES)

Watch the teaching video for session 3. Refer the group members to page 49 and remind them there is space to take notes.

GROUP DISCUSSION (11 MINUTES)

Refer to the Group Discussion questions on page 50 to stimulate discussion on the topics presented during the video teaching. Ask the group members to share any personal encouragement, challenge, or inspiration they received as they watched.

WRAP UP AND GO DEEPER (10 MINUTES)

Conclude by praying over your group. Review the schedule on page 54. Remind them to complete the personal studies before the next session.

OUR WALK

Pʀᴇᴠɪᴇᴡ ᴛʜᴇ ᴠɪᴅᴇᴏ before your meeting and complete all the written exercises in this guide. Familiarize yourself with the session outline and gather the necessary materials. Remember also to pray for the participants who will be attending.

SESSION OUTLINE
(60 MINUTES)

REVIEW OF PERSONAL STUDY (10 MINUTES)

Welcome any new participants, and then refer the group to their notes on pages 58–68. Begin by having several different members share the following:

- The lessons they learned from each verse (Step 3)
- The most meaningful question they wrote out in response to Step 4, citing the verse on which the question was based
- Their outstanding takeaway in Step 5

VIDEO TEACHING (30 MINUTES)

Watch the teaching video for session 4. Refer the group members to page 71 and remind them there is space to take notes.

GROUP DISCUSSION (10 MINUTES)

Refer to the Group Discussion questions on page 72 to stimulate discussion on the topics presented during the video teaching. Ask the group members to share any personal encouragement, challenge, or inspiration they received as they watched.

WRAP UP AND GO DEEPER (10 MINUTES)

Conclude by praying over your group. Review the schedule on page 76. Remind them to complete the personal studies before the next session.

OUR WORK

Pᴿᴇᴠɪᴇᴡ ᴛʜᴇ ᴠɪᴅᴇᴏ before your meeting and complete all the written exercises in this guide. Familiarize yourself with the session outline and gather the necessary materials. Remember also to pray for the participants who will be attending.

SESSION OUTLINE
(60 MINUTES)

REVIEW OF PERSONAL STUDY (10 MINUTES)

Welcome any new participants, and then refer the group to their notes on pages 80–90. Begin by having several different members share the following:

- The lessons they learned from each verse (Step 3)
- The most meaningful question they wrote out in response to Step 4, citing the verse on which the question was based
- Their outstanding takeaway in Step 5

VIDEO TEACHING (29 MINUTES)

Watch the teaching video for session 5. Refer the group members to page 93 and remind them there is space to take notes.

GROUP DISCUSSION (11 MINUTES)

Refer to the Group Discussion questions on page 94 to stimulate discussion on the topics presented during the video teaching. Ask the group members to share any personal encouragement, challenge, or inspiration they received as they watched.

WRAP UP AND GO DEEPER (10 MINUTES)

Conclude by praying over your group. Encourage your group to read the sections QUESTIONS YOU MAY HAVE and HOW TO BE A JESUS FOLLOWER on pages 113–122. Pray for each other as you choose to commit to being a Jesus Follower who passes on the Baton of Truth to the next generation.

QUESTIONS
YOU MAY HAVE
ABOUT BEING A JESUS FOLLOWER[2]

QUESTION—What is the most important characteristic of a Jesus Follower?

Anne:

You have to want to be a Jesus Follower. It starts in your heart. It is not something somebody can make you do. Or make you feel like you should do. To be a Jesus Follower is to be a Jesus lover and a glory giver. To love the Lord your God with all your heart and soul and strength. To want to be like Him. To want other people to be able to see Jesus in you, especially in the hard times. The trials are when you have an opportunity to love Him even more. He comes through in the most amazing ways.
For us to know that He loves us with all of His heart.

QUESTION—How can we motivate our children to read and study God's word daily?

Rachel-Ruth:

I think the biggest thing is to show them that you do it yourself and you love it. When we show our kids that we love studying our Bibles, that it's important to us, it's a priority in our life, then I think they will copy us. They do that in so many of the things they see us do, but that's the most important thing they can copy. I'm studying all the time. When they come into my study and sit down, I make sure that I have chairs for them where they can sit with me. And we often discuss what I'm studying. When

---

[2] The answers in this section were taken from a live Facebook interview.

your kids see that studying your Bible is important to you, then the hope is that it will become important to them because of your example.

Anne:

Reading and studying God's Word should not be a chore. I love the Scripture and I love sharing it with others . . . like something the Lord is saying to me through my personal devotional time in the morning. God's Word is living. He speaks through His Word. And if you can get that across to your children, it's no longer something they just check off as they learn facts and information. But they learn God is speaking to them, and it makes all the difference in their Bible reading and study.

QUESTION—How do we reach children who have learned or heard that belief in God is unimportant or irrelevant?

Rachel-Ruth:

The world wants to pull our kids away from God's Word and what the truth of God's Word is. They need to know what God's Word says, and I've taught my girls God's Scripture—what God says about these different issues that are hot topics in the world right now. Then when they go into school or spend time with their friends and they hear what's being taught or they hear what the kids are saying, they've been taught God's Word and know that's not true because they know God's Word is true. When you teach them, it sets the plumb line. It takes a lot to be a parent. It takes a lot of discipline yourself to make the time to teach your kids because we're busy, we're tired, we've got other things that we could be doing. If you choose to be a parent, you are choosing to make that your top priority because you're going to teach your kids and train them, disciple them so that they know God's Word, and are prepared when they step out and go into this world that is so separate from the Lord.

Anne:

The obvious thing is that in order to teach your children the truth, you need to know the truth . . . so you need to be in Scripture, in God's Word. There are so many sins today that are just mainstream. But if you read Scripture, do you know what the Scripture says about them? God's Word calls out those sins and says that they will not have a place in the kingdom of heaven. It's a very serious thing. Our standards have dropped to the point that because we compare ourselves with each other or the world around us, we have no standards. But God's standards haven't changed—so we need to know the truth. We need to be able to teach our children the truth. I remember my uncle once told me that we don't stand in judgment over God's Word. God's Word stands in judgment over us.

QUESTION—Is there anything you wish you had done differently to pass on the baton of faith to the next generation?

Anne:

There are many things I wish I had done differently in the past. But you can't drive forward by looking in the rearview mirror. You can have regrets from the past. You can beat yourself up over things that you didn't do right in the past. But that may ruin whatever God has for you in the future. I'm speaking to myself because I have some major failures in parenting. But the Lord has given me a release. I also know we can do everything perfectly as He does and still have a prodigal as He does. We are what we are by our own choices, and our children have to make their own choices. And so I would encourage you, if you're struggling with a child who is not living the way you raised them to live, it's not over yet. We judge everything by this point in time. But God sees the big picture, and He's still at work in your children's and your grandchildren's lives. I've seen answers to prayer that have taken years and years and years to receive. It's hard because it challenges our faith when we pray and pray for a child, and we don't see the answer. Then we can begin to question ourselves and question our prayer life. But just hang in there, keep praying, don't quit—the Lord hears, and He's awaiting that perfect time to answer.

QUESTION—How do we encourage teenagers to stand strong? How do you deal with friends who come to visit whose parents do not have the moral limits that you do?

Rachel-Ruth:

We have had a ton of kids in our home while my girls were growing up. And we faced many different situations. But I think the key, at least in our home, was that I had trained my daughters so that if a girl had come into the home who wasn't living for Jesus or wasn't taught the same way my girls were, then my girls would say something if necessary. It may have to do with the way they were speaking or what they wanted to read or watch. When it comes from your kid and they speak up to their peer in a sweet way, not in a condemning way—and they do it out of a heart of love—then it can make an impact. They just have to live for the Lord themselves, so pray and teach your kids to not be afraid to speak up.

Anne:

Sometimes as parents we want our children to be popular, and we want them to be accepted to the point that we're willing to compromise our values. And you can't do that at all. Your children may not be popular. They may be left out of everything. But to take the sting out of the rejection you can give them a substitute, an alternative that's more fun than what they would have done with their friends.

QUESTION—What are some ways to pass on our legacy when you are miles away?

Anne:

First on the list would have to be prayer. Then you can text or Facetime and you don't have to preach at them, but just let them know how God's blessing you and what He's taught you. To love our children, to listen to what they have to say, and then to look for ways that we can just drop seeds of truth into their hearts.

Rachel-Ruth:

If they are far away from you, you could ask them once a week if you could call and pray with them. Or ask them for prayer requests. Suggest they text or email their requests to you. Offer to pray with them over the phone. That lets them know that you think what they're going through is important, and you're willing to pray for them.

Anne:

And if you write down their prayer requests, then next week ask them how God answered. God will move in their lives. He will respond to your prayers on their behalf.

QUESTION—How do you advise guiding your high school and college-age children versus letting go of them?

Rachel-Ruth:

What I have tried to do is keep the lines of communication open where I'm not judging them and telling them no. At this stage it's so important . . . vital . . . to just love them. So take a deep breath and then love them and let them go. And God is the One who watches over them. He knows what's going on in their minds, what's going on in their apartments, what's going on with their friends . . . everything that we don't know. He knows how to walk them through that. He knows when to bring people into their lives. There's a transition we have as parents that is brutal. You just want them in your house. You want to direct them. You want to keep them under your control, but we have to let them go. At that point we just get on our knees, and we pray and pray and pray. God puts Scripture on your mind and lets you know at different times when you're supposed to say something or when you shouldn't. If you don't feel the quickening of the Holy Spirit, then don't say anything. Just wait until you feel the quickening of the Holy Spirit . . . and that's when you speak. God is an active God. He will help you as you parent His older children and pray for wisdom every single day. That is my number one prayer right now—*Lord give me wisdom.*

QUESTION—How do we show love to an older child who is continuing in sin without agreeing with her choices?

Anne:

Be a safe place. Then if your child asks for your counsel, certainly give it. But mostly listen. And once again, look for ways that you can just drop those little seedlings of truth into her/his heart. God's Word is like a landmine. You drop God's Word and plant it in somebody's heart—then the Holy Spirit comes along whenever He chooses, and He can explode the truth into faith so it makes an impact. God's Word is powerful. Maybe it would be a verse or something that you text. God can use His Word and your love to bring the prodigal home.

QUESTION—How do you not get discouraged about all of the wasted years and how they have affected our children and grandchildren?

Rachel-Ruth:

When there's a family gathering or something where you have your grandkids and your kids sitting around, just stand up, give them your testimony and tell them something like . . . "This is my life. There were times when I walked away from the Lord, and this is what happened. I shouldn't have, but this is where the Lord's brought me now. I love Jesus. He has changed my life. I wish I could go back and do it differently, but I can't. So I want to testify in front of you all and challenge you not to do that. Run with the Lord, walk with Him, read your Bible." Being honest with your kids and your grandkids while giving a testimony of your life can be absolutely transformative. Just say, I blew it.

When we start hiding things and acting like we had it all together, we did it right . . . that is the worst thing we can do. We're all a bunch of sinners. Be honest with your kids and tell them you've made mistakes and blown it sometimes, but now you're walking with Jesus. And this is the Scripture that brought me back to Him. This is the situation that God used in my life to restore a right relationship with Him. That's what's going to impact your kids, your grandkids, and they will never forget it.

Anne:

There's a precious promise in Joel, chapter two. God says that He will restore the years the locusts have eaten. In other words, the wasted years. So rather than cry over them or feel like such a failure—ask the Lord to restore to you those wasted years, and He can make up for it during the time you have left. You can still have a great impact on your children and your grandchildren. So just let Him make it up to you. But you can't do that if you don't surrender to Him. And I love the suggestion about sharing a testimony. If you can't gather them and do it in person, then do it on Facetime. Or write it down and send a written testimony to them.

QUESTION—If I messed up with my children, how do I make it up with grandchildren and share Jesus with them?

Anne:

The most important thing you can do, if you want to ignite faith in the next generation, is to be a person of faith. The most important thing you can do to get your children and your grandchildren to be Jesus Followers is to be a Jesus Follower. You need to be very authentic and very vibrant in your relationship with the Lord. So that's where I would start. I would start every day making time to pray and talk to Him. Read your Bible where you listen for Him to speak to you through His Word and talk to Him throughout the day. Look for things you can do to serve Him and develop that personal relationship with Him that's going to overflow in your family. They're going to see it.

QUESTION—I wasn't raised in a Christian home and don't know what a godly mother looks like. I don't have a godly example to follow. How can I know when I am setting a good example for my children?

Anne:

We are sharing this study with you to flesh out what it means to be a Jesus Follower as a parent and also as a child. We wrote this study for your encouragement that we could pull you into our family because we did have godly mothers and grandmothers. We just want to share with you stories so that our family heritage can be yours, too—and you could draw on our experience and what we've been through for yourself.

QUESTION—How did you share the gospel with your children?

Rachel-Ruth:

I remember holding all three of my girls in the hospital when they were born, laying there, just looking at their faces. And I shared the gospel with them. That was my first thing. I wanted them to hear it from me even if they didn't understand. I told them that Jesus loved them . . . that He died on the cross to take away their sins . . . and He could come into their lives and transform them. Then I would sing "Jesus Loves Me" . . . so that their newborn ears hear about Jesus and how He loves them.

But it wasn't until my girls were around the age of three that they each prayed, confessed their sin and asked Jesus into their hearts. Up until that point, every day I told them about Jesus and what He did on the cross for them. They were so familiar with the gospel that they each, on their own, asked me to pray with them to receive Jesus. It's important to talk about Jesus every day with your children as early as possible.

How to Become a Jesus Follower

FOR FIVE SESSIONS, you have been talking about and studying what it means to be a Jesus Follower. However, Rachel-Ruth and I wonder if perhaps we have made the assumption that you *are* a Jesus Follower. In the event you are unsure, we want to give you the opportunity to make that choice as you conclude this study. If you sincerely want to follow Jesus, pray this prayer:

Dear God,

I want to receive the Baton. I want to make sure I am in the Ark, saved from Your judgment. So right now, I come to the cross by faith and I confess I'm a sinner.[3] I was born that way. I'm a son of Adam. I'm a daughter of Eve. I'm asking You to forgive me of my sin as I turn away from it.[4] I claim the blood of Jesus to cover me, to cleanse me.[5] I ask that You forgive me in His name. And I believe Jesus died for me.[6] If there had been no one else who needed to be saved, He would have died just for me. I receive the Baton of Truth . . . the gospel . . . for myself. I believe Jesus rose up from the dead to give me eternal life which I understand is a personal relationship with You right now, and a heavenly Home when I die.[7] I open up my heart and I invite Jesus to come live inside of me in the person of the Holy Spirit.[8] I surrender my life to Him as Lord. From this

---

[3] Romans 3:23

[4] 1 John 1:9

[5] Ephesians 1:7

[6] Romans 5:8

[7] John 1:12

[8] Revelation 3:20; Hebrews 13:5–7

moment forward I will run my race, fixing my eyes on Jesus, following Him…all the way Home.

For the glory of His name,

Amen

If you prayed the above prayer in sincere faith, then your sins are forgiven! You have received eternal life! Heaven is your home! God is your Father! You are now an authentic Jesus Follower! You no longer have to struggle through life, running your race on your own! God is with you! He is for you! He loves you! You are now the Father's child! Welcome to His family![9]

We are rejoicing with the angels in Heaven,

Anne Graham Lotz   Rachel-Ruth Lotz Wright

Please visit our website to read more:
https://www.annegrahamlotz.org/jesus-gods-living-word/

---

[9] Excerpt from Jesus Followers

COMPANION BOOK TO ENRICH YOUR STUDY EXPERIENCE

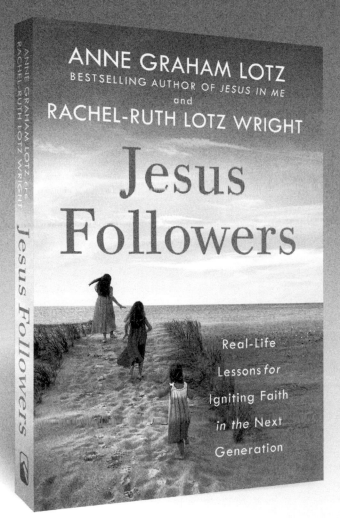

Available wherever books are sold

MULTNOMAH

Other Studies By
Anne Graham Lotz

DANIEL PRAYER STUDY GUIDE

In this study, Anne explains how we, too, can reverse the thunder until Heaven is moved and our own worlds change. Following the pattern of Daniel's original prayer, she helps us develop a more meaningful and powerful prayer life.

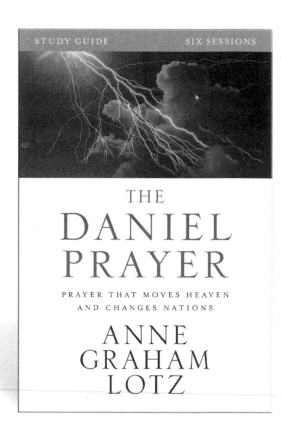

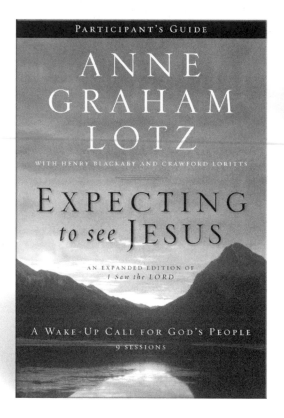

EXPECTING TO SEE JESUS PARTICIPANT'S GUIDE

In this nine-session small group Bible study, Anne Graham Lotz delivers a new message from the Mount of Olives in Israel and issues a wake-up call using the signs of Jesus' return.

JESUS IN ME

Through eight sessions, Anne will lead the way to revealing why the Holy Spirit is not an optional extra in the Christian life. Discover how you can better love and rely on the Holy Spirit—and embrace how much He loves you.

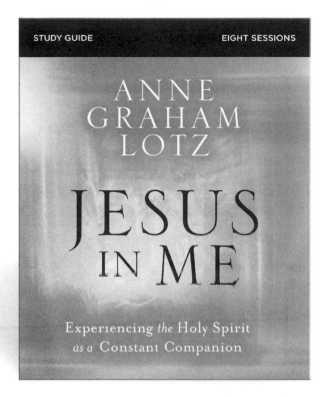

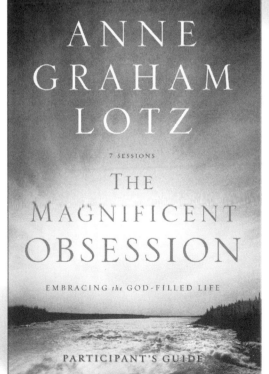

MAGNIFICENT OBSESSION

Follow author Anne Graham Lotz in this seven-session small group video Bible study, on a journey through Abraham's life, and learn—as he did—how to live a life of joy and purpose in the midst of struggle and doubt.